LS

A TRUE SPELL
AND A DANGEROUS

**Other Cambridge Reading books
you may enjoy**

Leopard on the Mountain
Ruskin Bond

Half of Nowhere
Richard Burns

Clyde's Leopard
Helen Dunmore

**Other books by Susan Price
you may enjoy**

Odin's Monster

Pedro

A True Spell
and a Dangerous

Susan Price

Illustrated with wood engravings
by Simon Brett

CAMBRIDGE
UNIVERSITY PRESS

Cambridge Reading

General Editors
Richard Brown and Kate Ruttle

Consultant Editor
Jean Glasberg

PUBLISHED BY THE PRESS SYNDICATE OF THE UNIVERSITY OF CAMBRIDGE
The Pitt Building, Trumpington Street, Cambridge CB2 1RP, United Kingdom

CAMBRIDGE UNIVERSITY PRESS
The Edinburgh Building, Cambridge CB2 2RU, United Kingdom
40 West 20th Street, New York, NY 10011-4211, USA
10 Stamford Road, Oakleigh, Melbourne 3166, Australia

Text © Susan Price 1998
Wood engravings © Simon Brett 1998

First published 1998
Reprinted 1998

Printed in the United Kingdom at the University Press, Cambridge

Typeset in Concorde

A catalogue record for this book is available from the British Library

ISBN 0 521 49764 7 paperback

CONTENTS

ONE

If Ruth turned the pages carelessly, they crumbled. The paper wasn't white, but pale brown, turning a much darker brown at its edges, as if the pages had been toasted. A smell like toast rose from them.

The book's hard green cover had been bleached yellow and white down one edge, as if it had lain in bright sunlight for a long time. Its pictures were wonderful. They were printed on a different kind of paper, which was smooth to touch, and their edges were still dazzlingly white. Each picture had a sheet of tissue-paper over it, to protect it, as if each one was precious.

The first showed a young man with long black hair and old-fashioned clothes walking between two small white deer. There were golden collars round the deer's necks, with a gold chain linking them together. Behind the man and the deer was a forest of green and blue trees. You could tell that it was trackless and wild. Under the picture, on the white border, in very black print, it said, 'True Thomas returns to the Land

Beyond.' Ruth had no idea what the words meant, but she liked thinking about them.

At the back of the book were several blank pages, their pale brown speckled with bits of the wood from which they'd been made. Their dark brown edges had crumbled. Someone had written on one of these pages, using very black, thick ink. When Ruth ran her fingers over the writing, she could feel the thickness of the ink. It must have been written long ago, because the ink was beginning to turn brown as well.

It took Ruth a long time to read what the words said, because they were in joined-up, careless, grown-up writing, very small and spiky. She'd had to concentrate hard and make a lot of guesses. As far as she could tell, the words said:

To see into the Land Beyond. A pint of sallet oyle and put it into a clean glasse. Put thereto the flowers, leaves and buddes of all flowers to be found in a place where faeries do wont to be. Set it to dissolve three days in the sunne, and then keepe it for thy use. Anoint thine eyes with it when thou dost wish to See. Be warned: this is a true spelle and a dangerous.

Ruth got up from where she was sitting on

the floor and went over to the window, taking the book with her. She knelt on the seat of a chair, and put the book down on the window-sill, open at the picture of True Thomas returning to the Land Beyond. Through the window she could see the garden.

There weren't any curtains at the window. They'd only moved into the house a couple of days ago. Many things were still in boxes, and rooms echoed oddly when you moved through them, because there were no carpets on the floor and no paper on the walls. Ruth didn't like the place much, but her mother told her she'd soon get used to it.

"Choose which room you'd like for your bedroom," her mother had said, and Ruth had chosen the room with the door in the corner by the window. She'd thought it would lead into another room, but when she opened it, there was just a small square cupboard behind it. Inside, on a shelf, the book had been lying, waiting for her, with its bleached cover and wonderful pictures.

"That's handy. It'll keep you quiet while I get on," her mother had said.

Ruth thought someone must have left the book specially for her to find. Only the night before her father had looked through the window and laughed and said, "There's fairies at the bottom of that garden!" And here in the back of the book was written a spell *to see into the Land Beyond.* The flowers used in it had to be picked from *a place where fairies do wont to be.* It was plain that someone had left the book for her so that she could use the spell.

Right outside the window was a little square of paving stones with a clothes line stretched across it. On the other side of the paving stones, a wilderness began. Tall grass, higher than Ruth's head; clumps of nettles; tall stands of willow-herb; straggly, thorny old rose bushes.

Masses of garden plants all tangled together with weeds and, at the back of the garden, standing higher than all the rest, a thick old hawthorn hedge.

She leaned on the chair back, watching the dense leaves and twigs shift in the breeze and thinking hard. *A pint of sallet oyle*, said the spell, *and put it into a clean glasse.* Sallet oyle must be something like salad dressing, she thought, and wrinkled her nose at the idea of mixing flowers up with that nasty white stuff. Or maybe it was something more like cooking oil? That made more sense to her. They were both called 'oil'. And there was a big bottle of cooking oil in the kitchen. Her mother wouldn't miss much of that – whereas salad dressing came in smallish bottles and it would be noticed if she took some.

She looked at the spell again. When she had her oil, she would have to put into it the flowers, buds and leaves of all the flowers to be found in the garden. Well, that would be easy enough.

Set it to dissolve three days in the sunne . . . That would be boring, having to wait for three days. And her mother might find it and ask her what she thought she was doing. Maybe she wouldn't need to wait three days? Maybe it would work right away?

But maybe you had to wait three days before the spell would work. Why would the spell say so otherwise?

Well, she could try and see. She could try it every day until it did work.

Anoint thine eyes with it when thou dost wish to See. She guessed that meant you had to put the flowery oil on your eyes when you wanted to see into the Land Beyond.

It was the last sentence of the spell that was most troubling: *Be warned: this is a true spelle and a dangerous*. That meant, she supposed, that it really would work, and that you would see frightening things.

She could hear her mother bumping around upstairs. Magic wasn't real, her mother said. The things that happened in Ruth's favourite stories, such as china ornaments coming to life at night, and animals talking, and magic tablecloths that served up food – none of these things could really happen. If she showed her mother the spell, her mother would say right away, without even thinking about it, that the spell was nonsense and wouldn't work.

Ruth wasn't so sure. Her mother was often right, but her mother and father also told her a lot of lies. They'd told her that her cat had run away, when really it had been killed by a car.

She climbed down from the chair and carefully put her book on the coffee table, where it wouldn't get dirtied with oil. She

went out into the hallway and stopped for a moment to listen to her mother upstairs. Her mother was busy and wouldn't bother her. She went into the kitchen.

Though the kitchen still felt strange and unlike home, it had a full set of cupboards and shelves, left by the last people to live in the house. The big bottle of cooking oil was standing at the edge of the dresser, near the cooker. Beside it was an empty milk-bottle, rinsed out and ready to be put on the step.

Put it into a clean glasse . . . The milk-bottle was clean and it was glass. Her mother wouldn't miss a milk-bottle as she would a drinking glass or a glass bowl. The bottle of cooking oil was big, and its outside was all sticky and slimy, so it was hard to handle. It was especially difficult to lift up the big heavy bottle in one hand while

holding the milk-bottle in the other. A stream of oil poured down the side of the bottle, over her hand and onto the dresser. It dripped slowly to the floor.

From upstairs her mother's voice called, "Ruth? Are you all right?"

"Yes!" she shouted back.

"Only you're very quiet down there."

"I'm reading my book," she shouted back, and held her breath until she heard her mother move away from the top of the stairs, back into the bedrooms. Her mother knew that she liked reading, so she probably wouldn't come to check up on her. All the same, Ruth hurriedly put the top back on the cooking oil and set it back exactly where it had been. She ripped sheets off the roll of kitchen-paper, mopped up the spilt oil, and then made sure that the greasy paper was stuffed well down in the plastic bag of rubbish.

Then she took the milk-bottle, half-full of oil, and went out by the kitchen door into the yard.

The sun had been shining brightly on the concrete flags for hours, and it was hot and dazzling. From the garden's tangle of greenery a pale pink rose leaned, and its scent drifted towards her, making her think of the hedge of roses that surrounded the Sleeping Beauty's castle. She pulled some petals from the rose and poked them inside the bottle, and then pushed in a sprig of rose leaves. But the fairies were wont to be at the bottom of the garden. Where was the bottom of the garden? The garden sloped up, so that the hawthorn hedge was on higher ground than the spot where she was standing. So she was at the bottom, wasn't she? Or was the end of the garden the bottom, whether it was higher or not? Perhaps she'd better put in flowers and leaves from all over the garden, to be sure.

She shouldered into the tall grass, following a path she had already made through it. The grass heads swayed, met and parted above her head, showering her with grains and dust. She pulled some leaves from them, setting them rustling, and poked the leaves into the bottle. Wrapping her hand in her T-shirt, she picked some nettle leaves without getting stung – much.

There were yellow roses and white roses, and big white daisies that had grown tall to reach the light, and all kinds of different flowers and leaves that she had no names for. From one part of the garden to another she went, pushing her way through tangles of stems, pausing to pinch through juicy green stalks or to snap woodier ones, and then to poke the sprigs down into her oil. Every now and again she'd put her hand over the bottle top and shake it hard.

It was hot, and she could hear bees buzzing. The air smelt of roses and grass. At last she found herself at the back – or bottom – of the garden, under the tall hawthorn hedge. The earth was damper there, in the hedge's shadow, and there was a smell of mud. She picked hawthorn leaves, and a couple of late hawthorn flowers, and pushed them into the oil. She shook the bottle up again, and slowly, holding her breath, smeared the oil from her thumb onto her eyelids.

She opened her eyes. Nothing had happened. She was still in the overgrown garden, under the hedge.

But perhaps the spell didn't work like that. Maybe the garden didn't change, but what you could see did. The spell, after all, was *to see into the Land Beyond.* She turned round, to see if she could catch any glimpse of the Land Beyond, or of any creature that might come from it. But all she could see were the tall weeds and sprawling rose bushes of the overgrown garden and, rising above them, the brickwork of neighbouring houses.

Oh well. The spell had said that the oil had to be set in the sun for three days before it would work. She would just have to wait. Where could she leave it?

The sunniest place was the little square of paving stones just in front of the house, but her parents would find the bottle if she left it there. They probably wouldn't take any notice of it, but, just to be sure, it would be safer to leave it somewhere else.

She stamped down a little circle of the tall grass, so that the sun came pouring down into the clearing she'd made. She stood the bottle in the centre of it. And there she left it.

TWO

The next day Ruth pushed her way through the long grass to where she'd left the bottle. Setting her hand over its opening, she shook it, and again smeared the oil on her eyelids.

Nothing changed. She still saw the dull roofs of the houses, the brick walls, and heard the sound of a neighbour's dog barking. She put the bottle back and left it.

The next day, the third day, she forgot the bottle until she was lying in bed and it was too late. Would the spell still work on the fourth day? She worried until she remembered that the spell said . . . *and then keepe it for thy use*. The next day, she thought, right after breakfast – or even before – she would try the oil again.

She had to wait until after breakfast. Her mother wouldn't let her go until she'd eaten, and the more she tried to hurry, the more her mother insisted on her having toast, and cereal, and orange juice. "Would you like an egg? Or an apple?"

She took an apple, to stop her mother pestering, and went outside, into the back yard, and into the tall, shifting grass of the garden. There, in the little clearing, she found the milk-bottle, leaning against its stone.

She finished her apple quickly, because she didn't want to get the sticky oil on that. Then she picked the bottle up and shook it, and peered inside. The leaves and flowers had shrunk into shiny black bits and pieces, saturated and limp with oil. She sniffed it, and took it away from her nose quickly. A thick, dank, rotten smell.

She sat among the tall grasses and crowded flowers, holding the bottle while the sun shone on her. She didn't want to put the stuff on her eyes, not when it smelt like that. But if she didn't, she'd never find out if the spell worked or not.

Be warned: this is a true spelle and a dangerous. Why 'dangerous'? What might happen? Perhaps she would meet – witches who would eat her, or dragons, or trolls. Her heart beat faster. She'd laughed at stories where trolls raged and exploded, or tore themselves in half – but she wouldn't like to meet a troll really. And, in stories, knights always killed dragons, but she wasn't a knight. She didn't have any armour or a spear.

Maybe it would be best to tip the oil away and not try it. Cowardly, though.

Well, I am a coward, she thought. I'm only a little girl. I don't want to get into trouble.

Coward.

Besides, it was only a game. She knew that really.

Go on, she dared herself. Go on. Try it.

Quickly, she stuck her thumb in the bottle, tipped it up, and then smeared the oil on her eyelids with two dabs.

When she opened her eyes it was, for a

moment, like looking through water. Everything wavered and shook. Then it settled, and she looked on trees. Tall trees, with thick, grooved trunks, and all their grooves grown with green moss. No houses, no roofs. Looking up, she saw branches, and leaves. Lowering her head, she saw tree trunks, and tall foxgloves, and brambles. Dust hung in the air, and fell from the trees above, and made all hazy.

Water was running somewhere, a cool sound. Apart from that small, liquid noise, there was a great silence, muffling her ears.

She rubbed at her eyes. Lifting the hem of her T-shirt, she scrubbed at her lids, trying to rid them of oil. She kept her eyes shut a moment longer and then, with another gasp, opened them. When she saw roses, and red brick walls, and heard a car passing on the road, she let out a long sigh.

But then she asked herself: had she really seen the forest, or only imagined it?

It had been too real to be imagination. She looked at her hands, which were scratched by brambles.

And, when she'd rubbed the oil off her eyes,

she'd come home again. So it was safe. If she met anything dangerous, a troll or a dragon, she could rub her eyes and escape.

She dipped her thumb in the oil again, and carefully put the bottle down. *Keepe it for thy use*. If she took it into the forest, she'd lose it.

She touched the oil to her eyes.

And opened them on the forest.

THREE

She took a step, and reached out to touch the bole of a tree. It was rough under her fingers. Old bark and moss crumbled from it, and it was cold to the touch, as live wood always is. Her feet moved in soft, deep leaf-litter, and the scent of it rose to her nose. A bramble caught her trouser leg, and clung, scratching her through the cloth. It is real, this place, she thought, as she stooped to untangle the thorns.

A rippling, bubbling sound of water came from somewhere nearby. She made towards it. A bird hopped from a branch, setting the branch swaying and leaves rustling while the bird flew away with a whirr of wings and a chattering cry of alarm. Ruth jumped, and stood still a moment.

At the bird's warning, the whole forest became still. Slowly she turned her head, looked into green-lit glades, peering into thickets, hoping that nothing was looking back at her. Nothing big, anyway. Nothing like a dragon – did dragons live in forests?

She couldn't see anything. But, she thought, you don't see them. They're camouflaged. They lurk and leap out on you . . .

She thought about wiping the oil from her eyes, but nothing big and clawed leapt snarling out of the bushes. I'll wait until something frightening happens, she thought. She moved on through the trees.

A thin little stream, brown as tea, was running between ferns, between rocks, between banks grown thick with starry moss. It made trickling noises as it was buckled into shining ripples by the rocks, and water-falling-into-water noises as it toppled over little falls. The smell of earth and leaves was richer there, by the water.

Following the stream wasn't always easy. Sometimes she had to crouch down to clamber over big boulders. Often the way was so steep and slippery, she had to leave it. Then she had

to push her way through trees and steep bracken before she could get back to the stream.

From the trees ahead came gruff coughing noises, and little yips. She stopped among the leaves, listening. There were thumps and scufflings, as if some kind of animal was jumping about. Slowly Ruth went forward, moving her feet carefully, setting her heel down first and rolling onto her toes, making as little noise in the fallen leaves as she could. When thickets blocked her way, she went round them, or gently moved branches aside with her hands, not letting them go until they were back in place. So she came to a place where she could look between tree trunks and leaves at a little grassy clearing by the stream.

There were five animals – three small ones and two larger ones. They had thick fur, which was greyish, but brownish too, and even black in places – but if she had been asked what colour they were, she would have said 'grey'. The animals had pointed ears, long snouts and thick, waving tails. They chased each other, nipped at each other and jumped over a fallen tree. The big ones rolled on their backs and let the little ones jump on top of them, and then leapt up, sending the little ones tumbling.

Ruth held her breath, but couldn't stop herself smiling as she watched. She watched every programme about wildlife and she knew wolves when she saw them. How *lucky*, she thought, how lucky I am.

She wasn't scared. A little nervous, but not scared. She knew from the programmes she'd watched, and her reading, that wolves weren't very fierce or dangerous to people. If she'd come across lions, or tigers, or bears, she would have been rubbing her eyes furiously. Since it was only wolves, she kept quiet and watched, and thought: I'm lucky.

One of the bigger wolves, chased by the puppies, ran right over the edge of the stream bank and landed in the water. There was a splash, a bark, and a wave of a long brown arm. Where the wolf had been, there now sat, laughing and splashing, a naked boy, who jumped to his feet, sending water flying, and threw onto the bank a wet and bundled wolf-skin.

The puppies yelped and scattered. The other big wolf sat down, wagged its tail, and wrinkled its nose in a wolf-laugh.

Ruth thought: werewolves! Clapping her hands to her mouth, she stepped sharply backwards. She bumped into branches, which set other branches swaying, and all the hanging leaves around her rustled.

The big wolf jumped to its feet, spinning to face her, its ears pricking up and its tail lifting above its back. The three little puppies ran behind it. The naked boy jumped from the water and landed in the grass on all fours. His head snapped round towards the trembling leaves.

The blue eyes of the wolf and the long dark eyes of the wolf-boy found Ruth where she stood among the bushes, and fixed on her in a long stare. She knew that they saw her. She almost felt their gaze hit her.

FOUR

Ruth turned and ran.

She forgot that all she had to do was wipe the oil from her eyes; and forgot that when you run from animals, it only makes them chase you.

She ran harder when the shaking and rattling of leaves and branches behind her told her that the werewolf and the wolf were after her.

It's hard to run in a forest. There are branches in your face all the time, and roots and briars around your feet, and the ground's full of unexpected hollows. As she desperately tried to keep lashing branches from her face, and look behind her, she didn't see the steep slope, hidden by bushes. She went sprawling and rolling over and over through juicy ferns, and sharp briars.

When she stopped rolling, she lay in a heap with all the breath knocked out of her, staring up at a whirl of leaves and branches against a blue sky.

Up the wolf came frisking. It thumped two big paws onto her chest, standing on her heavily, peering at her from its long-nosed face, from its big, clear blue eyes. It let its tongue loll from its mouth and panted, as if laughing. Its teeth looked so big and sharp-edged that Ruth was surprised its tongue wasn't cut on them.

There was more crashing and rustling in the ferns, and up came the boy who had been a wolf. He dropped down beside Ruth, hugged his knees and grinned at her. The wolf jumped over Ruth to the boy's side, where it shoved him onto his back, and stuck its long nose in his face.

The boy lay on his back and looked sideways at Ruth, still grinning. His teeth were sharp too, like a vampire's fangs, but not so long. His hair was brindled black and brown, twisted in wet curls. His eyes were the same bright brown as the stream, with no whites at all.

Those strange eyes reminded Ruth that if she rubbed the oil from her own eyes, she would be back in her own world, and safe. So, as the wolf and boy watched her, she rubbed hard at her eyes. When she still glimpsed the forest and the wolf, she licked her fingers and rubbed again, but it still didn't work. Grabbing at the hem of her T-shirt, she scrubbed at her eyes with that.

The wolf came towards her. "Don't bite me!" Ruth said.

The wolf put its whiskers and cold nose against her face, and licked her. It was tickly and wet and warm, and the wolf's breath smelt hot and meaty. Ruth could see the wolf-boy grinning at her from where he lay in the grass. His sharp teeth gave his smile a spiky merriment, as if he was smiling harder than ordinary people could. Water ran down his face from his wet hair.

Then the wolf shook itself and wasn't a wolf. A girl sat in the ferns with a grey wolf-skin across her knees. Grey hair hung to her shoulders, and her eyes were big and blue, with no white. She held out her hand to Ruth, and

Ruth took it, despite the long nails. She felt that these wolf-people weren't going to hurt her.

The wolf-girl got up, pulling Ruth to her feet, and led her back through the trees to the stream. The boy followed.

There were no wolves in the clearing now, but the girl led Ruth into the trees, until they came to a hollow sheltered and screened by leaves. There lay the three little cubs, hiding and waiting.

The wolf-girl and boy threw themselves down in the grass, their human skin all dappled with leaf-light and leaf-shade. The cubs wriggled and became small children, who jumped on the bigger boy and girl and hugged them because they'd been away.

They all looked up at Ruth, with dark eyes and bright blue eyes, but as she looked back at them, her sight wavered, as if she looked through tears. She blinked and saw the forest and the wolf-people clearly for a moment, but then it all shimmered, and there was red brick and tarmac.

Blinking again, she looked round, and was standing on a pavement of black tarmac beside a low garden wall of red brick. There were houses on both sides of the street, and cars passing. The only trees were small ones in gardens.

She didn't know where she was.

FIVE

A woman carrying bags of shopping was just turning into her gateway. Ruth asked her if she knew where Stokesay Road was, and the woman gave her directions.

Ruth went on, trying to remember when to turn left and when right. None of the streets looked familiar. They all had that bleak, cold look that streets have when you're a stranger. Even when she found a green and white sign reading 'Stokesay Road', she didn't recognise the street, and worried that she'd got the name wrong. Only when she was right outside her new house, and saw the number on the door, did she feel that she'd come to the right place.

She knocked loudly on the front door. It seemed a long wait before it opened. "Ruth, where have you been?" her mother asked.

"Nowhere."

"You've been somewhere. I didn't hear you go."

"I went for a walk."

34

"Well, wash your hands and come and have something to eat."

"I'm not hungry." Ruth squeezed past her mother and headed down the hall to the back door.

"Wash your hands and come and have something to eat."

"Can I just go out into the garden for – ?"

"No. You're going to have something to eat."

"But –"

"If I have any more argument, you're going to be in big trouble, my lady."

Ruth gave in. She washed her hands and ate tuna-fish sandwiches. "Now can I go and play?"

"Anything to keep you out of my hair," her mother said.

In the yard the afternoon sun was hot. Ruth dived into the long grass. All about her was a deep scent of hot earth and warmed leaves. The milk-bottle was where she'd left it, leaning against the stone. She picked it up, but then stood still, wondering.

The first time she'd used the oil, it had been easy to come back from the Land Beyond. The second time, it hadn't been so easy. What if it got harder every time? What if, in the end, she couldn't come back at all?

I don't care, she thought. I want to see the wolves.

She dabbed the oil on her eyes, rubbing it in well.

She opened her eyes and saw the forest's beautiful trees. From somewhere close came the sound of running water. If she found the stream again, and followed it, she would soon come to the place where she'd seen the wolf-people. This time she wouldn't be so frightened, and they would know her. It would be better, this time.

After a little wandering among the trees, she found the clearing by the stream. There was no sign of the wolves, and no sound of them either. She stood in the grassy space, listening, hearing the water running by her, and the leaves and twigs gently moving. Apart from that, there was a deep, vast silence.

Something at the edge of the clearing caught her eye. Thinking it was one of the grey wolves among the leaves, she went towards it, then saw it was no wolf, but a wolf-skin hung in the trees.

The breeze ruffled the shaggy hair, but the skin itself was too heavy to move.

She took the skin down. It was heavy, and smelt sharply of wolf. The fur was grey, brown and black, both soft and harsh to touch. The inner side was white and had the smooth, almost velvety feel of skin.

The skin had been left for her, she was sure. The wolf-people wrapped these skins around them and turned into wolves. They shrugged these skins off and became people. They'd left this skin for her so she could do the same.

She was wearing clothes. The wolf-people hadn't. She took off all her clothes and threw them down on the grass. Naked, she stood in the clearing, feeling the cool grass beneath her

bare feet, and the touch of the breeze on her
body, and she wrapped the wolf-skin round her.

The world changed.

It was as if she had suddenly crouched. She
saw the world from closer to the ground.

There was less colour. The greens, browns
and yellows of the forest bleached to grey, as if
the world had turned to a black and white film.
Everything that was still – such as the great
trunks of the trees – blurred and faded. But
every tiny movement, every flutter of a leaf in
the wind, every brushing of a leaf by a mouse,
seized her attention.

And there was more sound. What she had
thought silence was now full of scurryings and
squeaks and cries. Her scalp twitched as her

ears, now tall and pointed, shifted to catch each noise.

And smell. Raising her long pointed snout, she let the many layers of many smells drift across her wet nose, wondering at the savour of them all. She could smell the water of the stream, and the wet grass and other leaves that trailed in the water. She could smell the stones that the stream had wet but which were now drying. She could smell the mud at the stream's edge. The dry grass of the sun-warmed clearing had its own smell, and so did the earth. She could smell the different oils of the trees' leaves, and the trees' bark. And there were other smells – smells attached to those little shiftings and scurryings in the thickets. Warm smells of living

things: of fur, and blood, that made her hungry.

Smells that would guide her to the other wolf-people! She jumped up – and was astonished by the height and force of her spring.

She leapt and frisked alone in the clearing, discovering how strong and quick her new four-legged body was. Her spine bent and recoiled like a powerful spring. Her legs, as she landed and jumped again, seemed spring-loaded. She shook herself and the strong ripple ran down her spine, through her fur, and into her tail – a delicious feeling which she immediately repeated. She rolled on the grass, jumped up and rolled again. She ran and jumped into the stream, just for the pleasure of the splash, and of feeling her own strength as she leapt out again onto the grass. Then she lay down in the sun and panted. She liked being a wolf.

Getting up, she ran into the shade of the trees, enjoying the rapid trot of her four legs and the hard drumming of her paws on the ground. Her feet stirred the leaves underfoot, and new scents rose to her nose: the rich decay of leaves, the whiff of earthworms, the smell of mice. Leaves and branches, as she passed, brushed and

combed her thick fur, releasing new scents of sap and oils. Sounds filled her twitching ears: of her own passage, of birds in the branches above, little cries of alarm and running. Everything ran from her. She was a wolf. There was nothing in the forest she need fear.

It didn't matter if she let the whole forest know she was there. Throwing up her head, she let the wolf's howl rise from her throat, vibrating through her. She trembled as she heard it. The whole forest stilled but for the slight sound of the wind shifting leaves.

She waited a moment – and then was answered by other howls. The wolf-people were calling her. Here! Here! Here! Quavering, the calls rose and fell through the silence. Ruth – Wolf-Ruth – sprang to her feet and set off at a rapid, springing jog towards the sound of the calls. Sometimes she stopped and called again; sometimes the other wolves called to her.

They came, bounding through the trees, their tails waving high behind them. She felt the twitch along her spine as her own tail was hoisted to show her pleasure.

There was the young she-wolf with her grey coat and blue eyes; there was the boy-wolf with his brindled fur and dark eyes. They dashed against her and bowled her off her feet, rolled her over, nipping and snapping at her – but it was all in game.

Scrambling up, she nipped at them, and they chased each other round and round, rustling the bushes with their lashing tails, barking and yipping, glad to see each other again.

Then four bigger, older wolves came, and with them came the puppies. Ruth's friends, the boy-wolf and the young she-wolf, rushed to lick the older ones, and rolled on the ground before them. Ruth, seeing that this was the thing to do, copied them. The older wolves sniffed at her deeply, but then licked her ears, kissing her and welcoming her.

She was a member of the pack.

SIX

It was summer when Ruth joined the pack. The
trees hung heavy with leaves, casting the tracks
into deep, cool shadow.

The wolves' den was dug thirty feet deep into
the earth. Down there, deep underground, safe
and cool, the cubs and their mother slept
through the day.

The other wolves lay above, close by the den's
opening. Their grey and brindled shapes were
hard to see in the shifting leaf-light and shadow.
Every few minutes one or another would wake,
stretch, sniff the air and twitch ears, listening to
the forest. If there was nothing to cause alarm,
then the wolf lay down again and dozed for a
while.

But if one of the wolves gave a sharp,
coughing bark, all the others would sit up,
their ears pricked upright, noses sniffing.

At first the sounds, the smells, meant little
to Ruth. The three oldest wolves would rise,
stretch, and trot away to investigate. If Ruth
and the younger wolves tried to follow, the old

ones turned on them, laying back their ears and growling until the young ones lay flat. They were to stay on guard at the den.

The older wolves would soon come back, usually to lie down and sleep again. That meant there was nothing to fear.

If the old wolves came jogging back with tails waving, and jumped on the younger wolves, nipping them and rolling them in the leaves, then they had probably scented deer, to be hunted that night or the next. So Ruth learned the smell of deer.

Once, the old female wolf came back by herself, gathered together the young wolves with twitches of her ears and tail, and led them at a jog through the forest.

She led them to a steep place above a wide forest track, where the two old male wolves were waiting. They licked the faces of the young wolves as they came up, and then pointed to the track with their noses.

Ruth smelled the man before she saw him, and so learned the smell of mankind. She smelled his old clothes, and his sweat; the bread and cheese he was eating and the leather

of the old bag he carried his food in. She smelled the beer he had in a stone bottle.

Only when he moved did she pick out his shape with her eyes, from among all the shifting greys of branches and leaves. The man was looking nervously about him as he put a bite of bread to his mouth. He was alone, and frightened. He stared into the trees on the bank above him. The wolf-people peered back at him, but he didn't see them, or smell them.

Then the old male wolf leapt down from the bank onto the track. He reared up on his hind legs and turned into a brindle-haired, naked man, howling like a wolf and whirling a heavy grey wolf-skin in the air.

The man on the stone gave a loud shout and jumped up, throwing his bread and cheese one way, and his bottle of beer the other. He ran away up the track, crying, "Ah! Ah!" and leaving his leather bag lying in the dirt.

The wolf-people flourished their tails and barked, jumping down from the bank to meet the old wolf-man. Ruth wagged her tail and jumped up to lick his face with the others, and felt no pity for the man who had been chased away. He had been eating his dinner too close to the wolves' den.

The old wolf-man wrapped his skin about him again, and ran back to the den with them on four legs.

In the early evening, when the light was rich and yellow, and scents were sharp in the damp, cooling air, the mother-wolf led the cubs from the den. They ran among the older wolves, wagging their tails and lifting up their little faces to be licked.

Ruth and the two other youngsters played with the puppies and each other. They chased the cubs and let the cubs chase them: they leapt over each other, and knocked each other down and rolled each other about, until they were all exhausted.

The older wolves would join in for a little while, or would let themselves be stalked by the cubs, and jumped on and bitten, until a nip was too sharp. Then the big wolves would stand, shake themselves, and send the young ones sprawling, all long waving legs and tails. One big wolf would put a heavy paw on them and snarl – and to see those big teeth and those slitted eyes was scary, even in game.

As darkness came, thickening the shadow under the trees, the wolves sang. The smell of earth, leaves and water – and the ranker, sharper smell of fur-wrapped bodies full of blood – was stronger, and they knew they would soon have to hunt.

Any of them could begin the singing, even Ruth, even a cub. One of them would loose a long howl into the darkness, and another would join their voice to it, in a different key. One by one the whole pack would join, howling on a higher or lower note. It was their music, sung to raise their spirits for the night ahead. Ruth quickly learned to know the voices of them all: the two old male wolves, the mother-wolf and her old sister; and then Ruth's friends, the wolf-girl and the wolf-boy, and the three cubs. If they were separated, they could call to each other across miles of forest, and know each other, and come together again.

But when the oldest male wolf rose, looked at them all, pricked his ears, and jogged away, they knew the hunt had begun. They all fell silent, and rose, trotting after him.

Hunting was silent. Ruth learned that quickly. Once, in excitement, she lifted her nose and howled as the wolves trotted along a narrow forest trail. The wolf ahead of her, the old female, whipped round, her ears flat, her eyes slit, and snapped at Ruth's leg. The bite didn't break the skin, but it hurt. Ruth yelped.

All the wolves stopped. The old wolves came back and sniffed at Ruth with their ears laid back, their tails down and their eyes narrowed. Ruth lay on her belly and whimpered, hoping they would see she was sorry. Her friends, the youngsters, cringed low to the ground too.

Ruth rolled on her back like a puppy, to show the old wolves how sorry she was. They stooped down their heads, licked her face and ears, and went on. Ruth jumped up and ran after them. After that, she never broke hunting silence again.

But it was grand to hunt! To jog through the darkness with the damp air bringing every little, changing scent to her nose, catching quick whiffs of fear, her ears turning to hear the frantic scrabblings in the leaves as something small fled from their approach. Then they'd catch the smell of the deer they followed.

Ruth would feel her heart beat faster, and the fur move in her skin as she scented the deer and heard their small movements as they tried to hide themselves in the dark. She felt her own strength rippling down her sides from her shoulders, and felt the strength of her pack around her. But she kept the hunting silence.

They would come on the deer in some clearing, and see their moving shapes, black on grey. The wolves' ears and noses told them more about where the deer were than their eyes.

When the deer caught the wolf-smell, how they leapt, how they crashed through the

branches and juicy stems! Then Ruth felt the strength bunch in her shoulders, and her heart thump, the power of her muscles stretching her long legs as she bounded after with her friends. Their mouths gaped and they panted. With every hunt, they ran to their limits, because the deer were always faster. They could only catch the slow: the young, the old, the sick.

The fastest wolf, the bravest wolf, would leap and, if the leap had been judged right, lock its teeth in the deer's nose. The wolf would cling – the lock of a wolf's teeth is unbreakable – while the deer dashed on, dragging the wolf through thickets, bashing it against trees, scraping it along the ground.

While the deer was so held, the strongest wolf would leap and lock its jaws on the deer's hind leg or rump, and it was this wolf's strength that brought the deer down, though the other wolves would dash in, and bite, and help.

Once the deer was down, the wolf at its nose loosed hold, and bit again at the throat, opening the veins so the deer quickly bled to death.

Ruth ran with the rest, but when the time came to jump for the deer and bite, Ruth veered aside. She was only a young wolf, not as heavy or strong as the three leaders. The deer frightened her – its hooves were sharp as knife-blades. But young wolves were often afraid of the deer, and if her running had helped turn the deer towards the older, bigger wolves, then she had earned her share of the deer's flesh.

She ate with her family, pushing her head into the deer's warm body, biting the warm, soft, juicy meat with its iron taste. The mask of her face was red with blood until the other wolves licked her clean.

They ate until they were all crammed full, and then dragged what was left of the deer deep into the thickets. Slowly, heavily, they made their way back to the den, where they heaved up meat from their swollen bellies for the cubs, and for the mother-wolf, who had stayed behind to guard them.

The year had been turning colder, and the leaves all about them were red, yellow and russet. Old sister-wolf pounced off among the bushes to catch a large, struggling rat. She lay and played with it, holding it down with one big, grey paw, until the cubs had eaten, and then she let the rat go. Hurt as it was, it still tried to escape, but the cubs darted for it, bowling each other over in their eagerness to be its captor. They leapt high in the air, snatched the rat by its neck, shook it, threw it in the air, pounced on it and barked and threatened the other cubs who came near.

The old sister-wolf laughed, and Ruth saw that Sister had thrown back her skin and was sitting like a woman with a wolf-skin blanket round her shoulders. She watched the cubs playing with the rat, and laughed again.

Others were shrugging off their skins. They stood on two legs and stretched, and then lay down and rolled in the grass and lay at full length to watch the cubs. Ruth kept her skin on. She rested her nose on her paws, watched the

cubs pulling the rat between them, and listened to the wolf-people talk.

"Will you stay with us, Lost Child? Or will you go back to your own?"

Ruth knew they were talking to her, but didn't want to answer. Still in her wolf-shape, she went to play with the cubs, who were still throwing the now dead rat about.

The wolf-people were silent. Father said, "Her own kind won't take her back, now she's run with us."

"They'll cut her," said Sister, "with cold iron."

"Shoot her," said Mother, "with silver."

"You must stay with us, little one," said Brother, "and be safe." He pulled on his wolf-shape, rolled on his back and stretched out his front paws towards her, snapping his teeth and grinning.

Ruth was puzzled, but she thought hard about it all the next day, as the wolves dozed about the den. The wolf-people, she realised, thought that she was like the man they had chased away from his bread and cheese – a man of their own world, but one who had no wolf-shape.

Ruth herself found it hard to remember the world she really came from. She remembered making the oil with the flowers . . . She remembered the red bricks of the house where she had lived . . . More faintly, she remembered her mother and father. The memories were small, bright, distant pictures in her mind, quickly fading, like a dream already half-forgotten.

Soon she'd forget even those small, bright pictures. Now her mother and father had thick fur, and smelt of wolf.

If she stayed with them, one day she would be brave enough to leap and close her teeth on a deer's nose.

The trees were leafless, and the leaf-mould glittering with frost, when a braying of horns and banging of drums jolted them from their sleep. The wolves leapt up, shudders running through them. From the den Mother-Wolf came running, the cubs about her.

Hunters were in the forest. Hunters were coming to the den.

SEVEN

Mother-Wolf ran into the trees, followed by the cubs. Father lingered near the spot where they vanished into the leaves. His ears laid back, he listened to the hunters, ready to fight if need be, to keep them from following his family.

Sister turned on the youngsters and snarled at them, driving them away. They were to run and save themselves. The three young wolves scattered a little way, but turned back, afraid for their friends and the cubs. The banging of drums, the tramping of feet, were louder and closer.

Again Sister snarled, and this time the young wolves fled, plunging into the leaves that rattled and brushed against their sides.

All was a blur of grey before Ruth's eyes. Her legs stretched for every stride, her mouth gaping for breath, her heart thudding inside her. Sweat darkened and soaked her sides as she threw herself down steep banks and leapt and scrabbled her way up hills. Fur was torn from her, caught in briars. Her ears still twitched, even as she ran, catching shrill whistles and distant thumps on a drum.

A loud noise snapped close at her ears. Her front paw was snatched from under her and she fell. Jumping up to run on, she fell again. A tight grip held her paw, squeezing it. She couldn't move.

A log lay in the grass, and a split in the wood had closed on her paw. It was a trap. She jumped and jumped, trying to pull her paw free, but she was held too tight. The log was far too heavy for her to drag.

Her ears turned at the sound of movement close by. She smelt men, heard big flat, booted feet treading down the grass. Men had been hidden nearby, watching their trap. Now they were coming, no doubt with axes and knives.

Bracing two of her free feet against the log, she strained to drag her trapped paw loose, all the while hearing the shifting and treading as the men stooped under branches and pushed leaves aside.

Rub off the oil! Ducking her head, she rubbed her eyes on the fur of her legs, rubbing and rubbing. Still she could smell the forest, hear the hunters. An axe-head rang against a tree.

Frantically she licked at her fur, wetting it, and then rubbed her eye on it again. It wasn't working.

Every time she tried to rub off the oil, it was harder. Perhaps, this time, she couldn't go home.

A booted foot kicked the log. The stink of men was choking.

Through the grey of wolf-sight came flashes of green, russet, blue. The colours wavered, as if seen through water. The smells faded.

There was concrete under her knees.

EIGHT

Ruth saw orange brick, green grass, brown earth, a white washing-line post. In astonishment, she stared again, hardly knowing what to think or what she saw.

She thought, 'I'm back in – I'm back in – ' She couldn't think of the words she needed. 'I've come back to – '

She thought: The oil came off. I'm back home.

And then she thought: But my home is the pack. Not here.

She was safe from the hunt, but felt alone and scared, with ugly red brick all round her, and no other wolves nearby. The hunt was far away, and she was safe from it – but what if all the others were killed? Her heart beat even faster and more wildly than it had done at the coming of the hunt. She didn't want to be a lone wolf, without a pack.

When the hunt had passed, those wolves left alive would call to each other. Kneeling on the concrete path of a back yard, she howled because the brick walls and fences around her weren't forest trees. She needed to be in the forest, she had to be in the forest, to listen for her pack calling to each other. She had to be there, to answer and to go to them.

The oil.

Slowly, memories of the milk-bottle full of oil came back to her. She remembered the garden – very like this one – where she'd left it.

She stood, and stretched, her body feeling strange and long. It was hard to balance on these long straight legs, and she staggered as she took a few steps. It would be much easier to move as a wolf, and she would be much faster and stronger – but she didn't have her wolf-skin.

She realised she had nothing on. Among the wolves that hadn't mattered, but here . . .

Clothes were hanging on the line. There was a big blue shirt. She stood in front of it. Was it like a wolf-skin? If she put it on, would she become more human?

But if she was to move through this world, and find the milk-bottle of oil, she had to wear something. Unpegging the shirt, she put it on. It came almost to her feet, and she had to roll

the sleeves up a lot. Still barefoot, she padded
down the side of the house and into the street.

A door opened in a house on the other side
of the street. A woman came out and put
something in a big black bin that stood near
the door. Ruth had seen the woman before,
she knew she had. She watched the woman as
carefully as a wolf watches a mouse it means to
catch, until the woman went back into the
house and closed the door behind her.

She crossed the street, tottering as if she was
only just learning to walk. The steps up to the
front of the house were tricky and Ruth leaned
on her hands as she scampered up them. The
front door being closed, Ruth slipped round the
side of the house. The side-door was closed too,

and Ruth listened outside it. This girl's body
didn't have a wolf's sharp hearing, and its nose
made nothing of the scents all around. But,
even half-deaf and noseless, Ruth was sure
that the woman wasn't behind the door.

At the rear of the house was a tall patch of
weeds and flowers, a burst of green growth
between the surrounding walls. It was like a
little patch of her forest. Ruth knew it at once.
That was where she had left the bottle of oil.

Behind her was a window into the house.
Ruth looked in at it, ready to duck down out
of sight. The woman was inside, kneeling on
the floor, taking bundles out of boxes and
unwrapping them to reveal cups, bowls and
pans. The room around her was cluttered with
boxes, and chairs up-ended on each other, and
glasses and plates that had already been
unpacked.

Memories stirred in Ruth's head. This was the
house, out of all the houses, where she had used
to live. That was the woman who used to give
her food.

Get away! she thought. Quickly! Before she
sees you and traps you here. The pack would

call and call, but if she wasn't there to answer them, they might go deeper into the forest without her.

She looked over her shoulder at the patch of forest. She hoped it wouldn't take long to find the bottle of oil. Crossing the paving stones, she pushed her way into the overgrown grass and flowers. A trodden path showed the way she'd taken before. And there was the milk-bottle. It had been knocked over and most of the oil had been spilt. Never mind: there was some left in the bottom.

She picked the bottle up, stuck her thumb in the top of it, and carefully let enough oil run down the bottle's side to coat her thumb's end. She put the bottle down.

From the house came the sound of a window opening, and a woman's voice calling, "Ruth!"

The oil glistened on her thumb, and she remembered how hard it had been to wash the oil off her eyes when she'd been a wolf. It seemed that every time she used the spell, it was harder to come back from the forest.

"Ruth! Come here a minute!"

Ruth put her thumb to one eyelid and dabbed

the oil there. Through her open eye she still saw the pink roses of a nearby bush, and the red brick of the neighbouring house. Then she closed that eye and opened the other oiled one. She saw the forest, green and grey. She even caught the scent of its green leaves, water and earth. And a sound that might have been the dying of a wolf's howl.

She held her breath. Her heart felt squeezed. If she put the oil on her other eye, she would go into that forest, and she wanted to go there. She wanted to answer the wolves.

But was she certain – certain – that she never wanted to be human again, to walk upright, to use her hands? What if she ever needed to escape another hunt? Because if she went into the forest again, it would be harder than ever to leave it. She might never be able to leave it. There was no way of telling. It was a true spell, and this was its danger.

"Ruth! Are you going to come when I call you, or do I have to come and fetch you?"

Ruth showed her teeth. She rubbed the oil on her other eyelid.

When her eyes opened, the forest was around

her. Dust floated down through the air, shining in the light. Leaves shifted, whispering and dappling the green shade. But the forest was quiet. She could hear water running close by, but no drums were beating, no horns were blowing. The hunt was over.

Tipping back her head, she howled.

From around her, through the forest, came the calling and singing of the pack.

*The spell in this story is a real spell, taken
from a book of spells, or 'grimoire'.
Please do not try it at home.*